WONDERWISE™

Planes

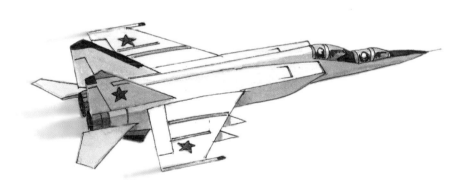

Published by Smart Apple Media,
an imprint of Black Rabbit Books
P.O. Box 3263, Mankato, Minnesota 56002
www.blackrabbitbooks.com

Published by arrangement with
The Salariya Book Company Ltd

Cataloging-in-Publication Data is available
from the Library of Congress

Printed in the United States
At Corporate Graphics,
North Mankato, Minnesota

9 8 7 6 5 4 3 2 1

ISBN: 978-1-62588-361-2

Illustrators: Mark Bergin
                Nick Hewetson
                Gerald Wood
                David Antram
                Tony Townsend

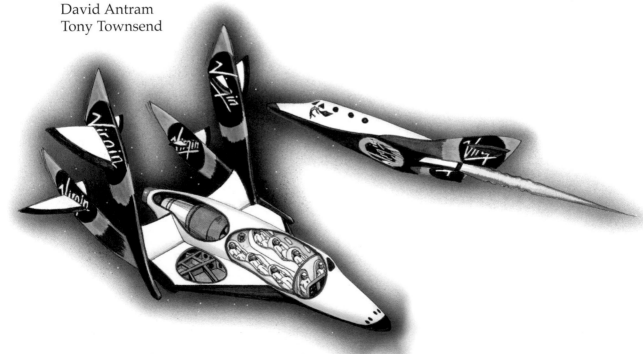

WONDERWISE
Planes

WILLIAM CAMERON

A+

Smart Apple Media

CONTENTS

INTRODUCTION

Planes are incredible flying machines. A large airliner weighs hundreds of tons and may carry more than its own weight in cargo, passengers, and fuel, yet it can fly through the air as if it weighs scarcely anything at all. Before planes were invented, people could only travel over land and water. But a plane can fly straight over rivers, oceans, and mountains making transport faster than ever before. Now it is hard to imagine a world without planes, as people fly from country to country in just a few hours.

LEARNING TO FLY

Flight has fascinated people for thousands of years. The first flights were made in balloons and gliders. These flying machines were carried through the air by wind power. Pilots could not fully control them though, so they could not be sure where they would end up!

► Medals were made to honor the brave German pilot, Otto Lilienthal.

▲ An ancient Greek tale tells us how Icarus flew with wings of wax and feathers. But the hot sun melted the wax and he fell into the sea.

▼ Otto Lilienthal was the first pilot. He flew only small gliders. By moving his legs he found that he could control these gliders.

◀ The first flying machine was a hot-air balloon. It was invented by the Montgolfier brothers and took off in Paris, France, in 1783.

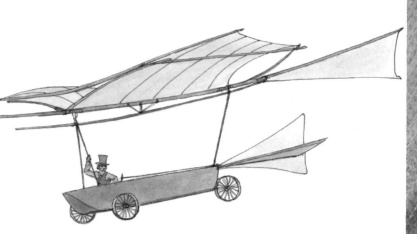

▲ Experimenting with gliders taught a British engineer named Sir George Cayley how the wings of a plane work.

EARLY PLANES

The wings of a plane lift it through the air. But a plane needs its own power to lift it off the ground and to give the pilot more control of the flight. In the first planes, this power came from an engine which turned a propeller. This pulled the plane forward. The first successful powered plane was the *Flyer*. Its first flight was on December 17 1903, and lasted 12 seconds. The plane traveled just under 130 feet (40 m).

▼ Orville Wright made the first plane flight. The plane was powered by a small, light, gasoline engine. He controlled the direction of the plane by leaning from side to side.

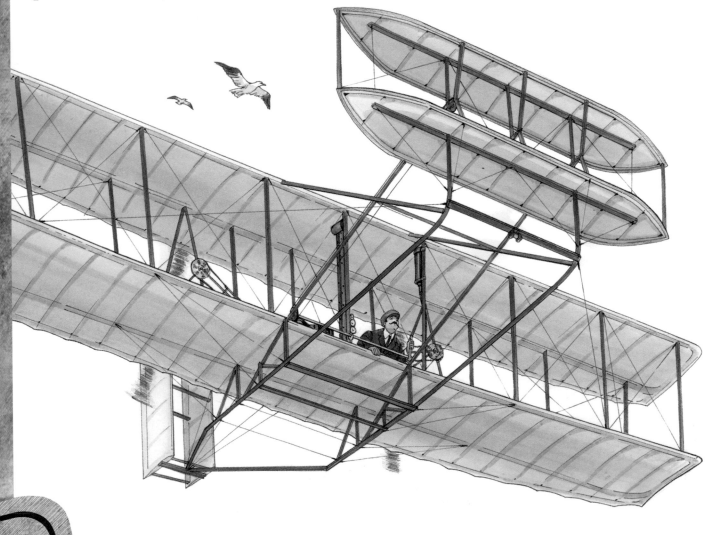

▶ Blériot's success made him very famous. Many people wanted to buy his plane.

◀ The *Flyer* was designed by two Americans, Orville and Wilbur Wright.

Pioneers, like the Wright brothers and Louis Blériot, made many models and had many accidents before they finally got off the ground.

▼ In 1909, Louis Blériot flew 23 miles (37 km) across the Channel from France to England. This was an important flight because people saw for themselves that planes were an exciting new way to travel.

▶ This medal was struck in Ohio after the Wrights' flight.

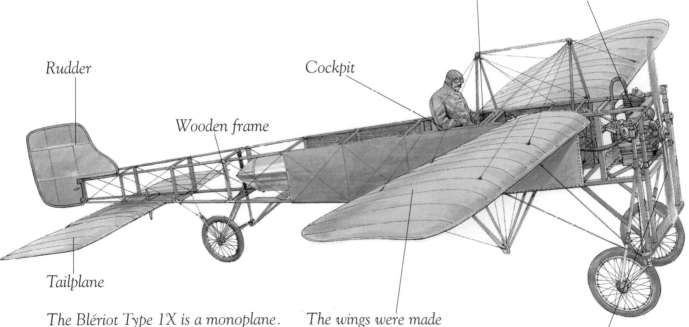

Control panel

Engine

Cockpit

Rudder

Wooden frame

Tailplane

The Blériot Type 1X is a monoplane. This means that it just has one wing.

The wings were made of wood and linen.

Propeller

SUPERSONIC FLIGHT

The fastest airliner was called Concorde. Most airliners fly at around 560–590 mph (900–950 kph), but Concorde had a cruising speed of 1,336 mph (2,150 kph) which is over twice the speed of sound. Planes that can fly faster than the speed of sound are called supersonic planes. Planes make a loud boom as they go over the speed of sound, which is called breaking the sound barrier.

Concorde was very fast but it was noisy. It was also expensive to run because its engines used so much fuel. In just one hour it would burn up 6,770 gallons (25,629 L) of fuel.

6060

▲ Chuck Yeager was the first pilot to fly faster than the speed of sound. He flew in a Bell X-1 rocket plane called *Glamorous Glennis*. The speed of sound is known as Mach 1. Twice the speed of sound is Mach 2.

Galley

British airways

Toilet

Flight deck

The cabin usually holds around 100 passengers.

The nose of the plane droops during take-off and landing to give the crew a clear view.

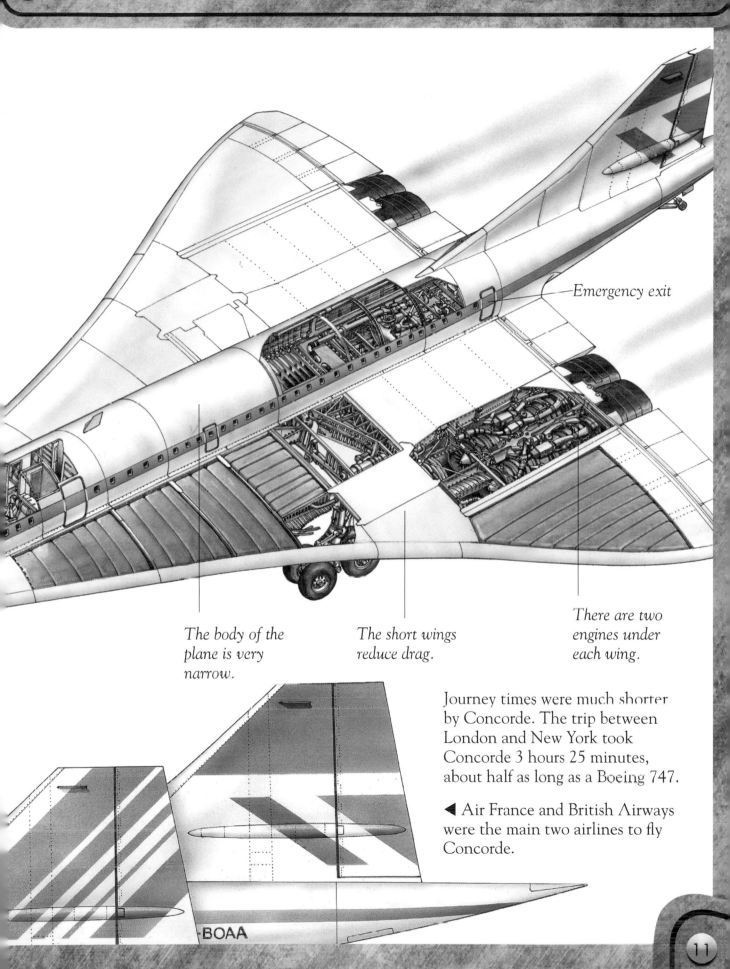

Emergency exit

The body of the plane is very narrow.

The short wings reduce drag.

There are two engines under each wing.

Journey times were much shorter by Concorde. The trip between London and New York took Concorde 3 hours 25 minutes, about half as long as a Boeing 747.

◀ Air France and British Airways were the main two airlines to fly Concorde.

G-BOAA

AT THE AIRPORT

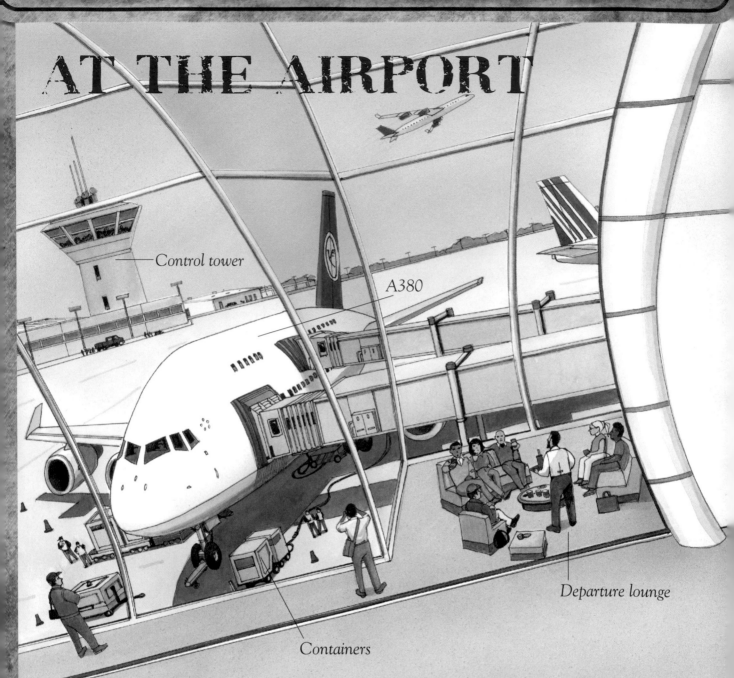

Control tower

A380

Departure lounge

Containers

Tugs move planes around the airport.

Before every flight the plane is prepared by the ground crew at the airport. Engineers check that the plane is in perfect working order. Other staff clean the plane inside and out, and stock it with everything that is needed for the next journey, from fuel to food. Meanwhile passengers have to go through airport security before boarding the plane.

Operators check the body scanners.

Metal detectors

Body scanners

X-ray

Airport security has increased dramatically since the September 11, 2001, terrorist attacks.

Baggage checks, metal screenings, and body scanners are used to ensure maximum security.

Trays for hand luggage

AIR TRAFFIC CONTROL

Flying in and out of the airport is the most dangerous part of a plane's journey, so the movement of every plane is planned by air traffic controllers. The planes on the ground are directed from a tower with a view of the whole airport. But planes in the air are tracked by radar. The controllers talk to the pilots by radio and give them routes in and out of the airport. At the world's busiest airports planes may be taking off and landing every 40 seconds, so the controllers' instructions are vital for safety.

Car parks

▶ A marshal directs the plane to the correct parking bay. Because a plane's engine makes so much noise, signals are made using bats.

Move forward

Over here

Turn left

Turn right

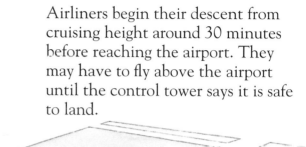
Stop

Stop engines

Airliners begin their descent from cruising height around 30 minutes before reaching the airport. They may have to fly above the airport until the control tower says it is safe to land.

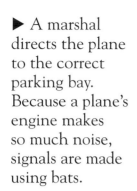

Passenger terminal

Apron (parking area)

The air traffic control tower tells the pilots when to move off.

The plane moves out of the parking bay. This is called taxiing.

The plane taxis to the waiting position and waits for instructions.

Permission to take off is given. The plane moves down the runway.

LIGHT AIRCRAFT

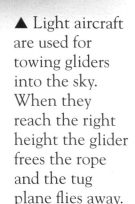

Small planes with an engine that drives a propeller are called light aircraft. They are slower than jet planes, but are much cheaper to run. They are useful because they do not need a big runway for take-off and landing. Light aircraft are used for training pilots and for local transport by people like flying doctors. These small planes can also be adapted to fight fires or spray crops.

▲ Light aircraft are used for towing gliders into the sky. When they reach the right height the glider frees the rope and the tug plane flies away.

▼ Amy Johnson set a new world record in 1930 when she flew from England to Australia in 17 days. Her plane was a small Gipsy Moth powered by just one engine.

Fuel tanks are built into the wings.

The DO 27 needs only a short runway. Some light aircraft can take off and land wherever there is an open space.

▼ *The DO 27 is a slow plane, but it is very sturdy and economical.*

The wing is set high on the plane. This gives the pilot a good all-round view.

The engine turns the propeller.

Elevator

Rudder

The propeller has a curved blade.

▲ The DO 27 was designed for all sorts of jobs. Some are fire-fighting planes. Others are used for training pilots, spraying crops, or for military duties.

FLYING BOATS

Flying boats are planes that use a lake or the sea as a runway. Except in bad weather, this makes them useful for flying between small islands where there are no runways. Today, flying boats are mostly very small planes, but in the 1920s and the 1930s, when few runways had been built, large flying boats were used as passenger planes.

▲ The first airliners could not carry enough fuel for long journeys. In 1938 one company airlifted a plane on the back of another plane. This meant that the plane could start its journey full of fuel already in the air.

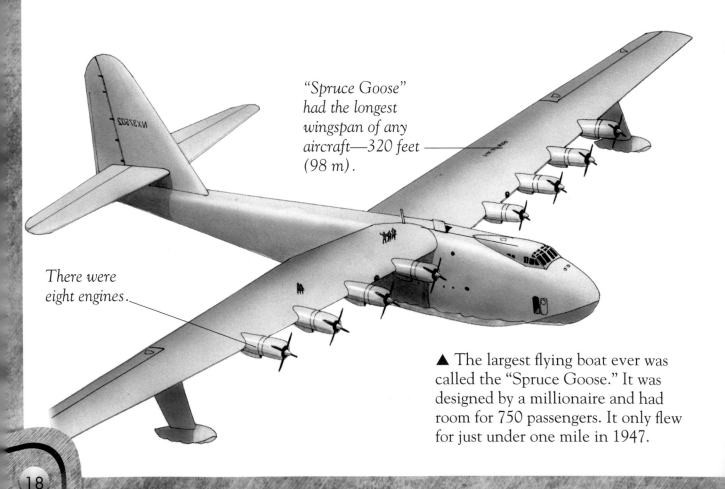

"Spruce Goose" had the longest wingspan of any aircraft—320 feet (98 m).

There were eight engines.

▲ The largest flying boat ever was called the "Spruce Goose." It was designed by a millionaire and had room for 750 passengers. It only flew for just under one mile in 1947.

▼ This flying boat was called an Empire Boat. It could carry up to 24 passengers as well as cargo. The largest flying boats could carry over 70 passengers.

The plane could be secured with an anchor, or moored in a harbor—just like a boat. Passengers boarded from a jetty or a motor launch. The wingtips were often supported by floats. These floats helped to stabilize the plane, especially as it landed.

The fuselage sat in the water, like the hull of a ship.

In World War Two, lots of runways were built for military planes. Later, passenger planes began to use these runways. This meant that flying boats—which were expensive to build and run—were used less and less.

JET PLANES

When the jet engine was invented, planes became much faster. Jet engines suck in air and blast out hot gases and this pushes the plane forward. Because jet planes fly so fast their shape is very important. It helps them to fly fast safely while using as little fuel as possible.

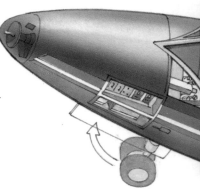

▲ The first flight by a jet-powered plane was in 1939. The plane was a German Heinkel He 178.

▼ Building an airliner costs millions of dollars. They are assembled in huge buildings called hangars. When the plane is finished, everything is tested thoroughly to check that is is working safely.

The engines are connected to the wing.

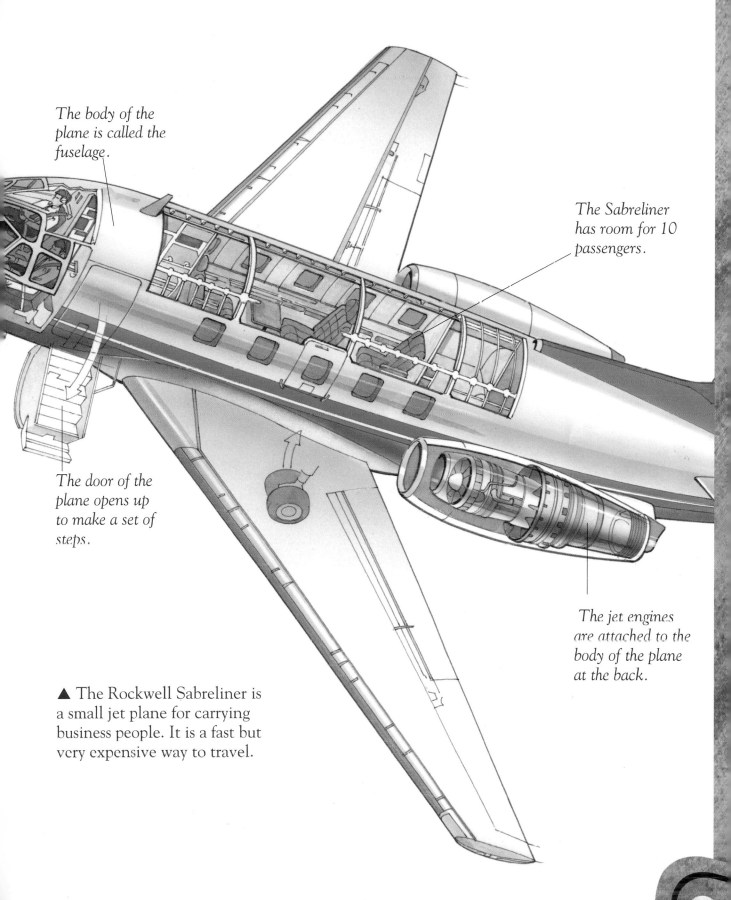

The body of the plane is called the fuselage.

The Sabreliner has room for 10 passengers.

The door of the plane opens up to make a set of steps.

The jet engines are attached to the body of the plane at the back.

▲ The Rockwell Sabreliner is a small jet plane for carrying business people. It is a fast but very expensive way to travel.

MODERN AIRCRAFT

Modern aircraft range in size and speed from double decker jet airliners to unmanned aerial vehicles such as the U.S. Drone.

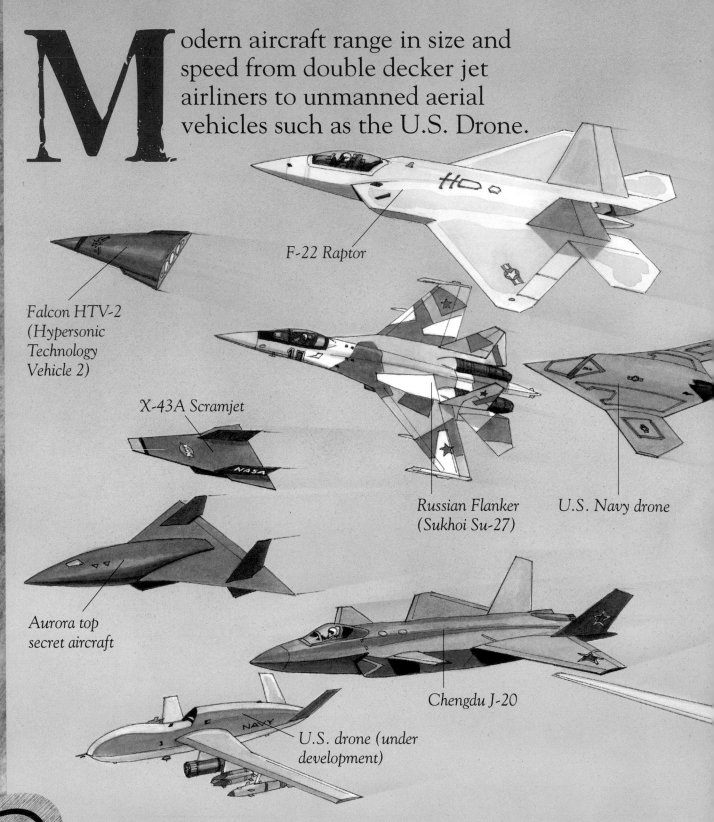

F-22 Raptor

Falcon HTV-2 (Hypersonic Technology Vehicle 2)

X-43A Scramjet

Russian Flanker (Sukhoi Su-27)

U.S. Navy drone

Aurora top secret aircraft

Chengdu J-20

U.S. drone (under development)

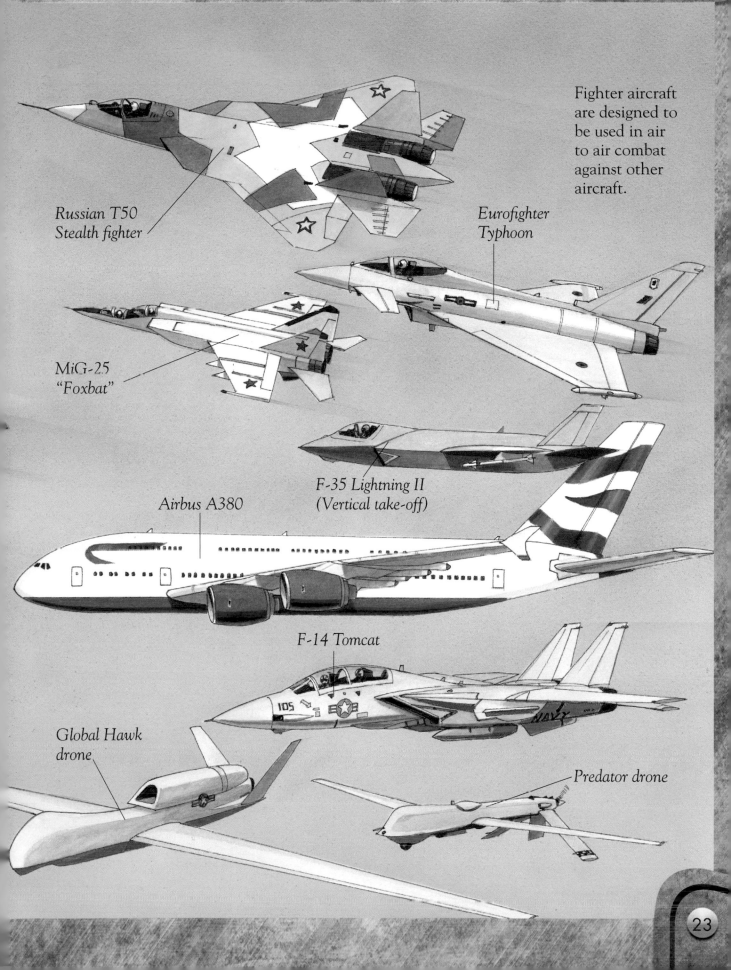

Fighter aircraft
are designed to
be used in air
to air combat
against other
aircraft.

Russian T50
Stealth fighter

Eurofighter
Typhoon

MiG-25
"Foxbat"

F-35 Lightning II
(Vertical take-off)

Airbus A380

F-14 Tomcat

Global Hawk
drone

Predator drone

THE PASSENGER CABIN

Large passenger planes fly millions of people all over the world each year. One of the most popular airliners is the Boeing 747. It is big enough to carry over 500 passengers and is also known as the jumbo jet. Passengers may spend many hours in the cabin of a plane so everything they need must be designed to fit into a small place.

The Boeing 747 has an upper cabin which holds up to 32 passengers.

Toilet

Baggage hold

Air stewards and stewardesses welcome the passengers on to the plane.

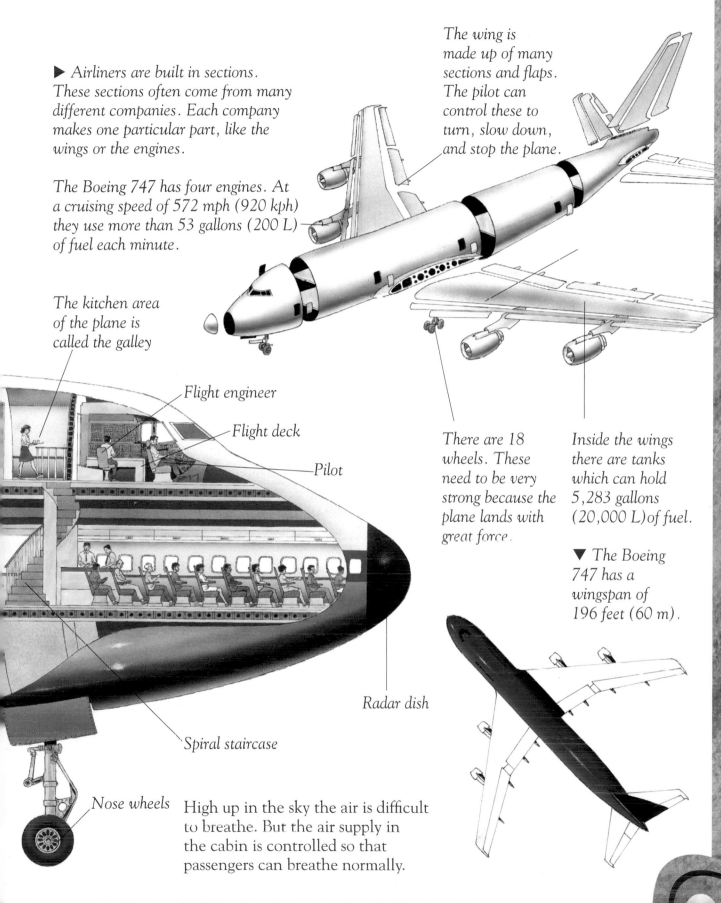

▶ Airliners are built in sections. These sections often come from many different companies. Each company makes one particular part, like the wings or the engines.

The Boeing 747 has four engines. At a cruising speed of 572 mph (920 kph) they use more than 53 gallons (200 L) of fuel each minute.

The wing is made up of many sections and flaps. The pilot can control these to turn, slow down, and stop the plane.

The kitchen area of the plane is called the galley

Flight engineer

Flight deck

Pilot

There are 18 wheels. These need to be very strong because the plane lands with great force.

Inside the wings there are tanks which can hold 5,283 gallons (20,000 L) of fuel.

▼ The Boeing 747 has a wingspan of 196 feet (60 m).

Radar dish

Spiral staircase

Nose wheels

High up in the sky the air is difficult to breathe. But the air supply in the cabin is controlled so that passengers can breathe normally.

ON THE FLIGHT DECK

▼ The flight deck is full of instruments that show the pilot how the plane is working. It also has radio equipment, and radar to give the pilot weather information.

An extra set of warning lights show the pilot if there is a problem with the plane.

A set of battery-powered flight instruments can be used if there is an electrical failure.

Dials show the pilot exactly how the engines are working.

The captain, the first officer, and sometimes the flight engineer, control the airliner. An airliner is a very complicated machine but the crew have computers to help them fly and navigate the plane. Although the crew constantly check the progress of the flight, a computer called an autopilot controls the plane for much of the journey.

▼ Information is displayed on screens in front of both pilots.

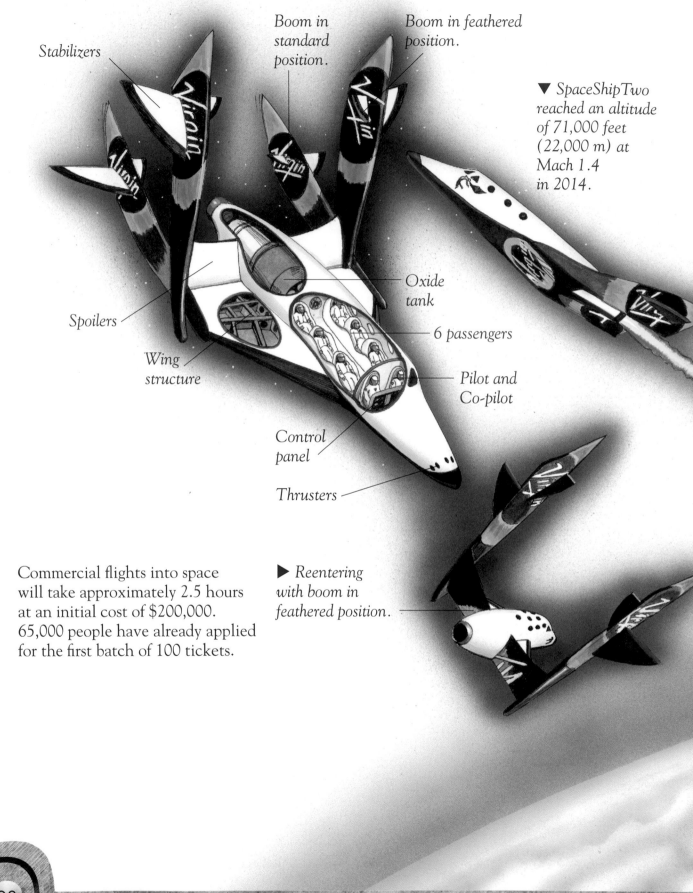

Stabilizers

Boom in standard position.

Boom in feathered position.

▼ *SpaceShipTwo reached an altitude of 71,000 feet (22,000 m) at Mach 1.4 in 2014.*

Spoilers

Wing structure

Oxide tank

6 passengers

Pilot and Co-pilot

Control panel

Thrusters

Commercial flights into space will take approximately 2.5 hours at an initial cost of $200,000. 65,000 people have already applied for the first batch of 100 tickets.

▶ *Reentering with boom in feathered position.*

SPACESHIPTWO

The SpaceShipTwo is an air-launched suborbital spaceplane. Built with the intention of one day taking tourists on brief trips into suborbital space.

SpaceShipTwo was unveiled to the public on December 7, 2009, in California.

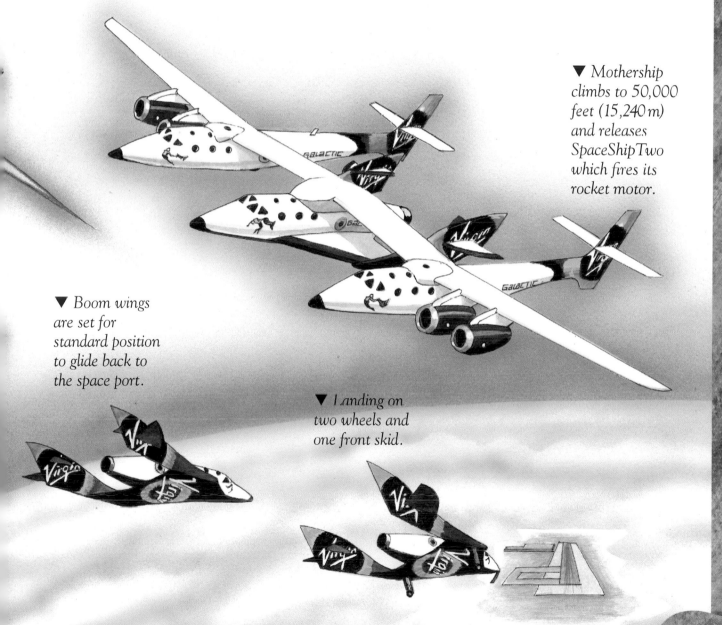

▼ *Mothership climbs to 50,000 feet (15,240 m) and releases SpaceShipTwo which fires its rocket motor.*

▼ *Boom wings are set for standard position to glide back to the space port.*

▼ *Landing on two wheels and one front skid.*

USEFUL WORDS

Cargo The goods carried by a plane or ship.

Cockpit The section of the plane that the pilot sits in.

Combat planes The many different types of plane used in war.

Cruising speed The speed at which a plane uses fuel most economically.

Drag The force that slows a plane down as it flies through the air.

Ejector seat A seat designed to shoot right out of the plane in an emergency.

Elevator A flap on the wing of a plane that is used to make the plane move up and down.

First World War The war involving many countries, which lasted from 1914–1918.

Fuselage The body of the plane.

Jetty A landing stage for a boat.

Mach Measurement of the speed of sound.

Propellers Curved blades that pull a plane forward when they turn quickly around.

Radar A system that uses radio waves to find objects like planes.

Rudder A flap at the back of the plane that is used to steer it.

Runway A large strip, usually made of concrete or tarmac, that planes use for take-off and landing.

Tailplane A small wing at the back of the plane that helps to keep it steady.

Terminal A building where a plane or train finishes its journey.

TIMELINE

c. 1000 BCE The ancient Greek tale of Icarus flying with wings of wax is written.

1783 Joseph and Etienne Montgolfier launch their first hot-air balloon.

c. 1850 Sir George Cayley carries out gliding experiments at his home in Yorkshire, England.

c. 1890 German engineer Otto Lilienthal successfully tests a series of monoplanes and biplane gliders.

1903 *Wright flyer* becomes the first aircraft to achieve sustained flight with a man on board.

1909 Louis Blériot successfully flies across the English Channel.

1930 Amy Johnson sets a new world record when she flies from England to Australia.

1947 Bell X-1 *Glamorous Glennis*, piloted by Charles Yeager, breaks the sound barrier, at a speed of Mach 1.015.

1969 First flight of the Aerospatiale Concorde supersonic airliner.

1974 First flight of the Airbus A300 wide-body jetliner.

1991 Lockheed F-117 is the first "stealth" aircraft used in combat during the Gulf War.

2013 SpaceShipTwo after nearly three years of unpowered testing successfully performs its first powered test flight.

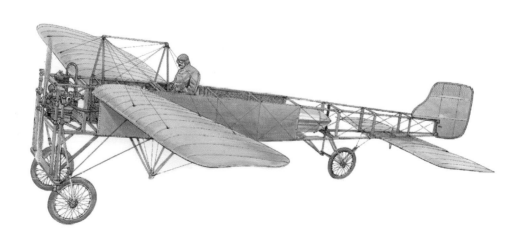

INDEX

A

airliner 5, 10, 15, 18, 20, 22, 25, 27
airport 12, 13, 14, 15
air traffic control 14, 15
autopilot 27

B

balloon 6, 7
Blériot 9
Blériot Type IX 9
Boeing 11, 24, 25

C

cabin 10, 24, 25
cargo 5, 19
Cayley, Sir George 7
cockpit 9
Concorde 10, 11

D

DO 27 17

E

engineer 7, 12, 25, 27

F

flight deck 10, 25, 26, 27
Flyer 8, 9
flying boat 18, 19

G

Gipsy Moth 16
Glamorous Glennis 10
glider 6, 7, 16
ground crew 12

H

Heinkel He 20

I

Icarus 6

J

jet engine 20, 21
Johnson, Amy 16
jumbo jet 24

L

Lilienthal, Otto 6

M

marshal 15

P

pilot 6, 8, 10, 14, 15, 16, 17, 25, 26, 27, 28
propeller 8, 9, 16, 17

R

radar 14, 25, 26
Rockwell Sabreliner 21
runway 15, 16, 17, 18, 19

S

SpaceShipTwo 28, 29
Spruce Goose 18

W

Wright, Orville and Wilbur 8